Su

scatterings of light and dark in poems, songs and essays

Flloyd Kennedy

LIVERPOOL

Copyright © 2020 by **Flloyd Kennedy**

All rights reserved. Except as permitted under current legislation no part of this work may be photocopied, stored in retrieval system, published, performed in public, adapted, broadcast, transmitted, recorded or reproduced in any form by any means, without the prior permission of the copyright owner, except for short quotes for the purpose of academic publications and reviews. All of the images, unless otherwise attributed, are by Flloyd Kennedy. For information, contact Flloyd Kennedy at flloyd@flloydkennedy.com.

Flloyd Kennedy
11 Heathcote Close
Liverpool, L7 6QA, Merseyside, UK
www.flloydkennedy.com
@flloydwith2ells
https://www.facebook.com/flloyd.kennedy
Bandcamp: https://flloydwith2ells.bandcamp.com/releases

Cover image: © Terry Cripps 2020 -- www.169.org.uk
Book Layout © 2017 BookDesignTemplates.com

Sunsets & Kites/ Flloyd Kennedy -- 1st ed.
ISBN 978-1-8381946-1-1

Dedication

To my beloved sons, Iain and Roderick, who continue to inspire and educate me as they have done for as long as I have known them.

Contents

I've Been Thinking... _____ 1
    What time is it? _____ 3
    I have a theory _____ 5
    Five point plan _____ 8
    Games of love and war _____ 11
    If I wanted to _____ 13

It's a Paradox... _____ 15
    Am I old yet? _____ 17
    — Coming, ready or not _____ 21
    Seventy-five not out _____ 24
    Grouchy Old Woman _____ 30
    Anatomy of despair _____ 41
    Mother William _____ 47

But I've Been Here Before... _____ 49
    View from Mt Coot-tha _____ 51
    Breathing out _____ 53
    My heart is in your keeping _____ 54
    I can hardly hear you _____ 55
    A dream _____ 56
    Obsession _____ 58
    In defence of the (so-called) Lying Cretan _____ 60
    For Iain - on the occasion of his 10th birthday _____ 63

Song Lyrics _____ 67
    The singing beetle _____ 69

Sometimes I think	73
The comeback queen gives herself a jolly good talking to	76
A loving hold	80
Merry go round of life	82
The good old days	87
Where the old folk go	90
The bottom line	92
Australia Fair no more	96
When I was a little girl	99
Sunsets and kites	103
About the Author	105
Acknowledgements	106

I've Been Thinking...

What time is it?

I am haunted by my present.

It ghosts me.

The past is a place that keeps me

From disappearing into non-existence.

We are always in the future.

Everything we see or hear

Has already occurred.

To others, we are always in the past.

No one is an island

But we are all alone nonetheless.

    And somewhere, always out of reach

    Because of course it's in the fourth dimension.

    There is an Anti-Matter Factory.

    There, clocks are made

    Defining that which doesn't matter.

    They tick and click each second into

    And out of existence

    In a single instant.

Here, in our earthly three dimensions,

We clutch at moments, hours, years

Tripping unknowingly through the seconds

Failing to celebrate each eventuality

Even as it dawns into being

And dissolves.

If I were a fly, living at speeds unimaginable

I would capture those seconds

Rich and random.

I would wonder at the sluggishness of humanity

Pondering aimlessly round and round

Always ignorant of the wonder

The magnificence of each unending

    Momentous, instantiated blending

    Of time, space, and what really matters ...

I have a theory

Big is not necessarily bold

More is not necessarily better

Growth is not necessarily healthy

Uncertainty is not necessarily

The same as insecurity

Borders are not necessarily threatening

    And democracy is not a system

    It's a process.

Men are not necessarily macho

Women are not necessarily caring

Gender is not a necessarily a status

Race is not necessarily a thing.

Variety is not necessarily the spice of life

Pain is not necessarily to be avoided

Novelty is not necessarily to be pursued

Sadness is not necessarily

The same as depression

    And democracy is not a system

    It's a process.

Beauty is not necessarily

In the eye of the beholder

Posing does not necessarily make you look good

Shouting does not necessarily make you bolder

Whispering cannot necessarily

Protect you from being found out

Worrying does not necessarily save the farm

Nor does worrying necessarily do any harm

    And democracy is not a system

    It's a process.

Two giant man babies playing in seclusion

Does not necessarily pose a threat

To world peace

Three giant man babies working in collusion

Does not necessarily mean life

As we know it will cease

Innumerable giant man babies

Afflicted with self-delusion

Does not necessarily require us all to acquiesce

In an end to democracy as we know it

Because democracy is not a system

Sufficient unto itself, that can be destroyed:

> It's a process, that continues
>
> Necessarily, if we all agree
>
> To work really, really hard at it.

Five point plan

The Alfa Theatre in Tel Aviv continues to work with both Israeli and Palestinian theatre artists under the direction of Professor Emeritus Avraham Oz, (Department of Hebrew and Comparative Literature, University of Haifa) in spite of having their grant funding severely restricted. Professor Oz had replied to my letter of support with the words "let us hope for better days".

Let us hope for better days

But in the meantime

Let me count the ways

We depend upon, to keep despair at bay.

>ONE: We dance.
>
>Our bodies move in time
>
>Rhythmically, a-rhythmically
>
>Refusing to accept declining
>
>Possibilities, whatever
>
>The degree of our abilities.
>
>We stumble and we fall
>
>With clumsiness and grace
>
>And we face the music artfully
>
>and then we dance some more.

TWO: We sing

Our voices ring

In the darkness, and the sound

May be sweet or grand or shrill

Sharing deep and silly dreams

Drowning out the chilly clamour

Of oppression, depression;

Music is our weapon.

THREE: We play

With wonder and with words

We share our wonderings

With generousity and creativity

With discipline and empathy

We challenge our communities

To wonder and to question

And we dare to do it with impunity.

FOUR: We share.

We come together

However we can

    Standing up and standing out

    Hope in our hearts

    Strength in our numbers

    Singers, dancers, writers

    Musicians, actors

    Claiming the right to be seen

    To be listened to.

Let us hope for better days

But in the meantime

FIVE: As a last resort –

And only, always, ever as a last resort -

    We fight

    for the right

    To continue

    To dance

    Sing

    Play And share.

Games of love and war

Those games of love and war

They tripped us up

They tore

The world apart.

Those games of love and

 Games of war

They tricked us all

      We swore

      We'd never start

      It all again.

   Those games of love and war

   Reveal the flaw

   That human nature tries to hide

   While mother nature

   Takes them in her stride.

      Those games of love and games of war

      They tripped us up

      They tore the world apart

Those games of love and war.

Games of war

Games of love

Who's to say what right we have

To fight

To play

With no idea of how we came

To be this way?

Who's to say it's time

To stop the game

Concede defeat

To run back home

And never come this way again?

If I wanted to

I could paint - if I wanted to.

Real arty-crafty stuff

You'd faint when you beheld my miracle

You'd flock in your millions.

You'd gasp—

Gasp in awe.

Women! The beauty!

Men would grin knowingly.

Full of perception

Proportion - deception

Misconception

No-one would ever know.

    I know.

        I would know.

It's a Paradox...

Angela Booth Photography

Am I old yet?

Coz I am starting to think

I've heard everything there is to hear

That I might already know

Everything that there is to know.

I don't mean that literally, of course.

I'm not that stupid.

I know enough to know that

There is always more to know

I just mean there is nothing on the radio

Or on the tv

That I haven't heard before.

Am I old yet? Because

I don't fear death. I fear pain.

And yet I experience pain all the time.

I fear that the pain will get worse

Till I cannot bear it.

And yet, each time it increases, I bear it.

And if I make it to 96

And you want to acknowledge

Any achievements I may have managed

Do not include being 96

Among my achievements.

Am I old yet?

Because sometimes

I feel a little bit lost.

But then I wonder

Is that even a thing?

What does it mean to be a 'little bit lost'?

Is it like being a little bit pregnant?

Or a little bit defrosted?

Am I old yet? I hear myself

Saying things my mother only started saying

When she was definitely old in my eyes.

Like "No! I don't want a new phone

With more computing power than a spaceship."

I don't want or need a cooker that talks to me

Or a washing machine that talks to the fridge.

I don't want to watch films or read books

About horrible people doing

Horrible things to each other

No matter how well made

Or well written they are.

Why would you?

Am I old yet?

Because I still have questions.

Such as: where does infinity start?

Where does it go?

How can you see the shadow of something

That cannot, itself, be seen?

Is there another life form on this planet

Quite as self-destructive as humanity?

Am I old yet?

My friends rush to reassure me that I'm not.

They are kind. I suspect they are afraid

That if I am old, they either are

Or soon will be, old too.

But I no longer dread discovering that I am old.

There is no law that says my 'old'

Will be the same

As my mother's. Or yours.

Any more than there was a law that said

My 'young' was the right

Or the wrong kind of 'young'.

Drifting between the event horizon

And the singularity

My body is a space ship, and

There is an end to the universe. It is

Out there, somewhere outside of

Me. And also inside of me.

And that, I think

Is probably, possibly

How old I am.

Five - ten - fifteen - twenty ... fifty-five... seventy -
— Coming, ready or not

Birthdays seem to arrive

At five yearly intervals these days.

No sooner do you celebrate fifty-five than

Sixty looms over the horizon.

Five years, or an instant

What's the difference?

Turning seventy-five was something

I viewed with

As much equanimity as I would the prospect of

Turning five again.

When I was five, we moved to Townsville

My mother, my sister and I.

My father was away somewhere on a boat.

(*Never a 'boat', mate! She's a ship!*)

We moved into a flat on the ground floor

Of an old apartment block

Right on the Strand.

One road to cross

Feet make friends

With warm white sand.

This is good.

My mother seems to like the place.

My sister is making friends.

I start school.

My first experience of mob rule

Peer pressure

On my first day.

Several assorted five and six year olds

Crowding round… Who knew who?

Another small child knew—

Chanting "I know your boyfriend!"

Joining in was a new experience

How alluring it seemed:

To be one of them

One of these strange

Exotic small people who knew each other

Knew strange exotic games

Knew how to enjoy them..

I hover on the edge of the crowd

I pick up the chant, get into the swing of it

Hear the bell in the distance

The call of the teacher

Feel the thwack of cane on palm

The next morning.

There is the added shame of being

Selected for special attention

Since the head teacher has been

Befriended by my very

Scary grandmother, in town on a visit.

My mother is not pleased.

Why would anyone want to be five again?

Now I'm seventy-five I am free

From the perceived necessity to be

One with others, and free—

If I keep working at it—

From the strange unease which is the

Price one pays for being asocial.

Seventy-five not out

At five, it wasn't all bad. There were dreamy moments when I was on my own and more or less content to be so, running with sandy toes to the swimming pool after school, dog-paddling aimlessly in the late afternoon sun, wondering how to do the dangerous, splashy things the other kids were enjoying so loudly down at the deep end, feeling that unease, the sense of inadequacy; wandering, (dawdling, as my mother put it) back along the now cool pavement, warm sandy air blowing aimlessly in my way and I'm dreaming heroic, fantastical dreams of leaping loudly from the high board. Those were the days (whack! "You're late again"), those were the days alright (whack! "What time do you call this?" Whack!)

What happens to time when you are a child? Apparently, nothing that doesn't happen when you grow up. It passes you by, overtakes you, sneaks around you like a thief in the night, turning 'five to' into 'five pasts' before you can blink. My mother would try to be reasonable. ("Come home at four"). I arrive at five past four. (Whack! "Come home at four fifteen"). I arrive at twenty past. (Whack! "Do you think I enjoy this?" Whack! "You must think I'm stupid!" Whack! "Do you want another smack?" Whack!) Don't be a mother if you can't handle irony.

Don't cry, that's not how it works. Screw your face up, breathe in, pretend you are over it, save your breath, save it up for later, all those thousands of sharp intakes of breath will pour out in one brief but all-encompassing flood half a century later as the coffin leaves the church, my two tall sons following – and that's no way to say goodbye to your father.

When I was five, I could read. I don't remember learning to read. My mother assures me I learnt to read by sitting on her and my father's knees and learning the words as they were repeated to me. I have no recollection of this. I do remember the letters of the alphabet on the big panel over the blackboard at school. How fascinating that these wonderful shapes have names of their own. I should have waited. Being able to read precludes the possibility of sitting on anyone's knees and being read to.

Reading a story to my cousin Lloyd kept him still for whole minutes at a time. Otherwise, we play in the backyard, recreating the cowboy movies we watch on Saturday mornings. ("I'm Roy Rogers!") Oh, ok, that means I'm the old guy, the dopey one, what's his name… Hayes? Shaggy Hayes, Baggy Hayes? Now I see I was a character actress in the making. Or maybe a clown.

Lloyd is a leader, a boy wonder and a dare devil. He can tight rope walk along the top of our fence. Hey – I can do it too! Lloyd taught me how to ride a bike, as a reward for being his faithful side-kick, the slow-witted Sergeant Lampard to his intrepid Inspector West. Lloyd used to run away from home. Sitting in the classroom, the teacher would turn on the radio and there would be the announcer – "Here is a special announcement. A six/seven/eight year old boy has gone missing. He was last seen wearing…" and I would know it was Lloyd. My father used to run away. First when he was fourteen, he ran away to sea. Then, whenever he got bored, or had a new idea, or had to get out of town, he would be gone again. When I was fifteen he disappeared at sea. I was convinced he was just running away again, that he would turn up in a year or so as he always had. After a while, I gave up. Years later, I said goodbye to him in the middle of the Indian Ocean, and it is quite possible that there is no good or bad way to say goodbye to your father.

Once, and only once, my cousin Lloyd invited me to play truant with him from Sunday School. We loped up Castle Hill, along the foot worn path under a hedge, and played inconsequential games while I tried to persuade him that running away was not a good idea. There was nothing in my experience which could justify such extreme action. I knew nothing then of his alcoholic father, the beatings, and he did not enlighten me. My mother's occasional wallop with the coat hanger or the hem ruler was just what mothers did as far as I was concerned. Whack! Unacceptable behaviour will be punished. All in all, I did not particularly enjoy the truanting experience, the guilt and fear of retribution which accompanied the whole event, but I did – I do – so want to know what it feels like to be outrageously naughty, to actually deserve the reputation I seem to have acquired at school ("You're a Ring Leader!") A Ring Leader! Leading the Ring into danger, into wickedness, into Fun! If only…

It is a great puzzlement to me that my inability to keep my mouth shut and my opinions to myself should be interpreted by those in authority as the worst form of leadership qualities, those which only ever result in dire consequences for those lead. At boarding school my reputation seemed to have preceded me, for they knew I was not the girl my sister was. She was good, she worked hard. I was not, and I did not. How easily such myths are made. School remained for me a place where books and stories and ideas were made available and constructed. All you had to do in return was what they asked of you, and they gave you more. What was there to work on? Why the constant "could do better's" and "doesn't work hard enough's"? I had no idea that I was allowed to venture beyond the given and explore for myself. Everything outside of the books was confusion and unease.

Other girls collected in the yard, or in the dormitory in groups, whispering and giggling, strange exotic creatures who knew each other, knew mysterious places and spoke in riddles. I hovered on the edge of several groups, still trying to figure out what was so much fun about splashing about in the deep end. Dangerous schemes were concocted, like midnight escapes over the back fence to collect some weird fruit which tasted abominable when they shared it out before breakfast. They were always caught, and so was I, whether I had been there or not, because apparently, I was the Ring Leader. The injustice rankled, and still I felt guilty, knowing I had to play along, because loyalty to your 'mates' meant taking the blame for them. ("Never, ever carry the can back for anyone, mate!") The only advice my father ever gave me, and I couldn't do as he asked. Confusion, unease, guilt. Why would anyone want to be seven again?

Gabby Hayes! How could I forget that name? The old dopey guy with the messy beard and hair, the silly hat, the squeaky voice. He was so comfortable with his baggy, dusty clothes and his idiosyncrasies, so quick to laugh at his own foolishness, so loyal. Hey ho. Maybe I was seven by then.

When I turned seventy, I didn't mind having been sixty. My sixty-year old friends seem like young halflings, while I still haven't learnt to stop saying "It's a generation thing". I wore silly hats and baggy dusty clothes and I was comfortable with my idiosyncrasies and I laughed at my own foolishness. But I did not, do not understand those halflings who insist that I am glamourous.

My mother had a glamourous friend when I was seven. Her name was Joan Rutherford, and she wore red. Her hair was black, her stiletto shoes were black, and her straight skirts and tailored jackets and lips and long sharp nails were red. She probably never wore tailored jackets, this was Townsville and 1951 after all, but in my child's eye she is Joan Crawford, and I am terrified of her. One day, I came in from school and my mother and Miss Rutherford were sitting at the kitchen table, drinking wine, and giggling. My mother told some story about how Joan had suggested that they buy some wine, and how it tasted 'off', but that's because that is how claret tastes! I stood inside the kitchen door, pretending that this was just like any other day, my mother sharing her day's activities with my sister and me, giggling, but in fact my mother did not share her life, or drink wine, or giggle. Laughter happened to her sometimes. Sometimes laughter would bubble around her and she would catch it, like a short sweet virus. Once, I made a tea party with little plastic cups and saucers, set it out on the back steps, and invited her to come, to play with me. ("I'm too old to play"). Did she really say that? I thought I was too old for toy teacups, if the truth were told, but I was determined to have at least one experience of my mother playing with me, the way the mothers in the story books did. It took a few goes, back of the throat held hard in case, but I persisted, and she came, and sat with me, and laughter happened. I pretended that this was just like any other day, and it was — all the days were pretended.

No, I don't want to be five again. Seventy-five is fine. It's not the same as sixty-five, because I save money on the hair dye I was using at fifty-five, pretending I was still forty-five. My mother gave up commenting negatively on my hair colour since I took the time and effort to train her, in her late nineties, to be more circumspect, but my sons may. My mother learnt to laugh and share her day's activities with me, but my sons have not, not yet. By the time my mother learned how to hear me, to be comfortable to share her own confusions with me, I realised that my sons must have a mother who lives in the secret recesses of their minds and hearts, and who is a stranger to me. Their memories of her are inaccessible to me and I may neither know nor understand them. My mother was astonished and hurt when I recalled events of our lives from my childhood perspective. Gradually, as I aged I discovered the possibility of exploring some sort of mutual understanding with her. Perhaps there is a shift in our perceptions which only becomes possible after seventy, and I was just lucky that she was still around to share the experience with me. If that is so, I can't wait to be eighty, so that my sons complete my training..

Grouchy Old Woman

Part I

Lives alone

By choice, and yet

No choice.

Because years ago they

Decided to live separately

And then he died anyway.

A kind of unintentional suicide

Because that is what alcohol does.

It comes into your life

Disguised as personal choice

The dis-inhibitor releasing joy

While silently gnawing at your spirit—

Quaffable spirits, tasty and heart-warming

Depleting all the life-sustaining

Chemistry of your soul

Until your organs cannot access it any more.

Still on her own. Grouch-old woman.

Who raised her children to not need her

Who misunderstood what it is to be needed

Who thought needing meant controlling

Who thought needing meant

Unhealthy attachment

Who confused independence

With self-sufficiency

And so they grew up independent

And self-sufficient

Without any need for her in their lives

While she needs them to at least

Need her

To be needed.

Part II

Her bedroom is beginning to resemble

Her kitchen table.

Cluttered with stuff for creating

For making, formulating

Ideas for the taking, half-baked

Ready to prove

When the temperature is right

That she is not without worth—

Not without a use that the world

With all its hurly-burly

Could find a place for.

A trace of her humanity

Might be

Just what the world's

Creative seed bank needs.

Her thoughts could be seeded

In perpetuity -

Not in the dark cold refrigerated unit

That resides in the northern wastes of her brain

But in the warm, life-generating

Cellular repository

Of joyful regeneration

Where every dumb idea

Is dumped into the streaming force

Of a larger phenomenon collider

And left there until one astonishing

Bosonic particle leaps out

Fully fledged

Phoenix-like

Magnified in beauty and delight

By the very impossibility

Of its existence.

But would it still need her?

Grumpily, grouchily

She considers that very real

Possibility.

Do ideas, like children

Lose their need for the originating mind

Once they transform into action

Form their own transactions

Across time and space?

Once they have left the incubator

Human or mechanical

Once they have found their feet

Begun to dream their own dreams

Aspiring to be more real, more maniacally

Self-sufficient, creating families of their own?

Probably.

Groucho-like, she determines

The supreme idiocy

Of all such thoughts

Returns to contemplating

Why the bedroom has acquired

The accoutrements of a work place

Why the sacred resting place - where

"Death's second self"[1] should reign supreme—

Bears little trace of peace and quiet

Festooned as it is with cables

---

[1] from Sonnet 73, William Shakespeare

Screens, books, recording devices

All instruments of torture

To a troubled soul.

Whom no one actually needs.

What does she actually need?

She needs to get out more.

She needs to finish SOMETHING.

Even if it's just this poem.

She needs to share some ideas

Release them

Set them free to grow up

Make demands and have needs of their own.

To experiment with points of view

And attitudes, perhaps demanditudes—

Which don't exist

Unless you make them so.

She'll reach out to the world at large

For other people's lives

And ways of thinking.

The radio reeks with righteous and

Considered conversations

The TV roars with outrage and injustice

Real and fantasised.

Sadness wells, springs from un-primed

Artesian bores

Gushing with uncalled for tears—

And for what purpose?

Who needs it?

So much empathetic sadness, for tragedies

Near and far

And nowhere to put it.

Such a waste.

In days gone by the tears were rare

A powerful rage would set her feet a-marching

Along with the tribe

The like-minded angry – and young

Protesting feet.

The feet could stand the pace.

Now the rage, like her face

Is lined and sunken, its power

Invisibly Ingrained

Deep inside her bones

Those bones whose joints will not suffer

Too much exertion.

And so, with every new disaster

Each reiteration of ongoing and obscene

Injustice, tears flow, and slowly reveal

A different form of unfamiliar

Power.

How to understand it?

How to tame it, frame it into

Something useful?

That takes time, and time is

Not necessarily in plentiful supply.

It will take patience—

Even less of that to spare —

It will take commitment.

It will take great self-control

Resisting the (almost) over-whelming urge

To leave with a punch line.

She isn't leaving. Not yet.

There is nowhere to go

Why would you leave

If there is nowhere to go?

Everywhere she has ever been

Every somewhere has also proved

Itself to be a another nowhere.

And vice versa. "Here, There and

Everywhere"[2] used to be her favourite

Song. And still is. Nothing changes

While everything changes.

Moving on doesn't have to mean

Moving out.

---

[2] The Beatles

Part III

Backpack slung jauntily across her shoulder

Fully loaded iPad inside, primed with

Murderous women.

How times have changed.

Screens that used to drip with

Mutilated female bodies

Deadly deconstructions

For and by male gazing eyes

Now glisten with bright

But not too bright

Or it would all be over in one night

Female seekers-after-justice

And their prey

The fabulously flawed

Lady killers—

Ladies who will drill an ice pick

Into your eye if you so much as

Look at them.

Viciousness

Allied with vacuous-ness

The antidotal reaction

To all that fabled niceness of a former age

(Was it really? Really?

Were people ever that nice

Kind, courteous, generous?

Probably not).

She trails a wheeled suitcase

Towards the station

A spring in her step

That wasn't there yesterday.

She's on the move

With plans, open minded

Wild hearted schemes

Simmering gently, wafting their

Aromatic smog around her brain.

Anatomy of despair

This time, there will be no – what's the word?

Reprieve.

She was about to say

'Relent' but

Knew it was wrong.

By a fluke the

Appropriate term

Surfaced in the nick of time.

Somewhere in the charnel house

That is her brain

A kindly, soulless neuron

Sifts through the detritus

To retrieve the lost word.

But this is digression.

There is no reprieve.

No stepping back

From the need

To take up the knife

Dissect the corpse

Begin the process of

—what's the word?

Here we go again.

She knows what it is

Just can't name it:

That thing that happens when

The death has no known cause.

In this cold, hopeless case

It's Hope itself that has died.

And the tag

On the toe of the corpse reads

"Despair".

But what's the name of this

Morbid process

So desperate to enact itself?

The splitting open of the corpse

Revealing its gory innards

Twisted and curling

Slackly, inert, offering no insights

Merely dry analysis.

Forensics?

Something to do with forensics.

There is no point in persisting

In this tedious insistence

On finding the right word.

The effort of senselessly seeking

Without finding

Exemplifies

The state of Despair.

Always it comes back to Despair.

Even though the death of Hope

Would seem to confirm that there's

No point, any longer, in looking.

And yet — for as long as she keeps looking

Hope cannot be quite dead.

So Despair

Cannot be the lifeless remains

Of what was once an animated Hope

After all.

Despair must be Hope

That is very, very unwell!

Thus Despair anatomised

Reveals itself as Hope in disguise

A masked intruder who claims to be

The devil incarnate and then turns out to be

A court jester jangling the alarm

Speaking truth to power.

"You're in despair?" sneers the jester.

"You've lost all hope?

Then why are you still here?

How are you coming up with all these

Clever-clog analogies if you've

Given up hope?"

She turns to face the jester

Sees herself in the mirror

Recognises herself

Even though the image is reversed

Because—

She has only ever seen herself

Reflected

In silvered glass

Or others' eyes.

A backwards look at particles of light

Deflected nano seconds into the past.

She cannot know, for sure

How she appears in the world, because—

Just as she has now learnt that

Despair is really Hope in reversal

Rather than its corpse—

Who and what she is in the world

Is always a shifting

Time consumed reflection

Of what she feels like

On the inside –

AUTOPSY!

It's called an autopsy.

Ha!

Might as well laugh at herself as cry.

They do use the same muscles, after all.

Mother William

I am old, Mother William

The lady cried.

And she cried, and she cried

And the windy sails turned

And her white head was burled

Inside out, upside down

Upside down, inside out

Why return? Asked the wind

And the sand and the tide.

I returned to be here.

I was here,

I was here...

I am old, Mother William

The lady cried.

You were old yesterday

Sang the wind and the tide

And the windy sails burned

And her old heart was turned

Inside out, upside down

Upside down, inside out.

I returned to be here.

I was here.

I am here

With the wind

And the sand

And the tide.

But I've Been Here Before...

View from Mt Coot-tha

(*Brisbane. Qld*)

North

    Towards childhood

    Longing – looking back

    At possibilities and memories

    The broad panorama encompassing

    My dreams.

South

    To mystery. Mountains

    Dissolving in mists. Other people

    Go there to live, to dream

    To populate its fragility.

    I watch. I visit. I return

    Do not touch.

    Mystery dissolves.

West

    Setting sun spreads its wide wings

    Over the land.

    Landing out west, my people

Spread like demented ants

Excoriating what they did not recognise.

Beguiled by the land, the sun

Folds its wings

In the bosom of a wild and

Furious shelter.

East

Beyond all imaginings.

Tantalising. Challenging. Beckoning.

Breathing out

Breathing out is good for me

But so is being held

Not to make the sadness go away

      That's my job.

And let the hold be real

Or virtual

I will feel your love

Within my bones

Keeping me warm

And safe

And calm

And still

While the movement goes on

So that I can keep on

      Breathing out.

My heart is in your keeping

My heart is in your keeping

And you know it not.

My heart with yours is sleeping.

It nestles, quite unnoticed

Breathes with your warm breath

Skips a beat when you are afraid

Ticks on, and on, and on

Through the day's routine.

I am obliged to you for the racing

And the pacing.

My heart is in your keeping

Whether you know it not.

I can hardly hear you

I can hardly hear you

Barely, beneath my skin

I feel your name

And know you.

There is no sense in it.

I should be drunk to be so stupid.

So what price this hard won right

Not to judge myself

Turn it out, not in.

A dream

I dreamt I spoke with your voice.

Your thoughts, unbidden and

Unwarranted, sprang from my mouth.

My head was crammed with your dreams

Your fantasies snaked around my heart.

My feelings lodged within your arms

Your blood ran deep and red throughout my veins.

My lungs breathed out your songs

Your lips and tongue ate my repast.

My belly gorged on your sufficiency

Your sleep encompassed my dreams.

I dreamt you wished with my soul.

My spirit laughed with your tears

Your sighs proclaimed my needs.

My life gave up your ghost

You gave up my love.

I dreamt I spoke with your voice.

I spoke of dreams beyond desire.

Your voice inspired desire

Beyond inspiration.

Beyond inspiration

Is the sound of your voice

In my dream.

Obsession

I think of you.

That's all I do.

Every waking moment of my life.

I read something, and I hear

Your voice — just a phrase

An echo in my mind, so clear.

I walk down the street

And you are there, in a shop doorway

Crossing the road, driving past

Buying a book, looking at shirts.

In the kitchen, I chide myself

For eating cheese, which you don't like.

I'm not doing it consciously you understand.

It happens to me.

You — are happening to me.

Not that it's really you.

If it were you, we'd hardly

Be having this conversation.

Not that this is a conversation.

If it were really you

For one thing, you'd be doing all the talking

And it would be about yourself

Your work, your friends

Your life, your beliefs.

You're a self-opinionated bastard.

No?

Are you interrupting me?

Do you have the temerity to speak for yourself

In my fantasy?

Good.

Now you can talk some sense into me.

Then I'll be cured.

In defence of the (so-called) Lying Cretan

(in which a person from the island of Crete states that he is lying. But if he is lying, then he is telling the truth, and vice versa - how can this be?)

To The Editor
Aegean Times
Piraeus

Sir

With regard to the headline of your recent article (*The problem of the Lying Cretan)* I wish to make it clear to your readers that I take great exception to the assertion that the esteemed actor Epimenides (of Crete, descendant of one of our most honoured philosophers) is a liar.

When he made the statement "I am (now) lying" Epimenides was not lying. On the contrary, he was expressing himself truthfully, with poetic licence. This rhetorical device has been used since the days of Aeschylus to great effect in poetry and drama. Epimenides, consummate artist as he is, instinctively incorporates this into his improvisations.

According to your literal interpretation, when Epimenides said "I am (now) lying" he was stating a fact, and a fact is by definition true, in which case he was lying. By this reasoning it is also possible to say that if he were telling the truth, then the statement must be both true AND false. However, it is impossible to speak truthfully and tell a lie at the same time (a lie being an intentionally false statement and the opposite to telling the truth). Therefore, his statement could not be both true and false.

This being the case, the statement must be neither true nor false. But this is equally impossible for the same reason, that one cannot lie and speak truthfully at the same time. So if Epimenides was stating a fact, we are left with the ridiculous paradox that his statement was both true and false, or neither true nor false.

When Shakespeare's Hamlet utters the words "I am dead, Horatio" (*Hamlet,* Act V sc ii), he is not actually dead. If he were he would be unable to speak at all. Yet he is speaking sincerely, without intent to deceive. It would appear that the statement "I am dead, Horatio" is not literally true, it is not a 'fact', but when spoken truthfully in the circumstances of his status and condition, states a higher Truth — the Truth, in fact, that his aspirations, intentions and princely potential are finished, along with his life. The words epitomise the desolation of the moment at the climax of the play. As the late distinguished Scots theatre director Tom Fleming stated with reference to a similar line in *Macbeth (*Boy: "He has killed me, Mother", Act IV sc ii), it is not a lie. It is poetic licence.

Yet if Hamlet's words could not, given the same or similar circumstances, be spoken by any one of us, then Shakespeare has failed as a dramatist. Had he failed we would not still be watching productions of his plays, especially *Hamlet*. He succeeds because his characters do speak for us, expressing our deepest desires and sorrows, only with greater effect. Shakespeare's skill lies in the way he uses language, and one of the devices he uses is poetic licence — the freedom allowed to writers in regard to grammatical construction, and to the use of facts, "especially for effect" (*Australian Concise Oxford Dictionary*, 3rd ed. [1997] p 1035)

When Mr Epimenides said "I am (now) lying", like Hamlet he is referring to a greater truth than the literal meaning of the words. He was engaged in the telling of a tall tale which grew taller by the minute, until he reached the point where his remark "I am (now) lying" was the epitome of exaggeration. Just as Hamlet's use of the present tense ("I am") heightens our awareness of the wasteful tragedy of his death, so Epimenides's "I am" heightens our awareness of the gargantuan nature of his fabrications, and of our complicity in them. Hamlet's "dead" overwhelms us with the inevitability of loss. Epimenides's "lying" generates universes of make-believe. "I am dead" in Hamlet's mouth makes us aware of our own mortality in a moment of catharsis. "I am lying" slipping from Epimenides's tongue awakens us to the vitality of our own imagination and playfulness.

Thus Mr Epimenides was not lying. He was speaking truthfully, through the device of poetic licence, expressing in the fewest possible words not so much a simple fact as the greater truth of humanity's endless capacity for invention.

I remain

Yours faithfully

Apallina of Athens.

For Iain - on the occasion of his 10th birthday

When Iain Alasdair Kennedy

Was very nearly one

He didn't care for Teddies

But he loved to suck his thumb.

And then when he was nearly two

He learned to bake a scone

And when he tried to eat a bit

The whole darn thing was gone!

When nearly three he learned that he

Could ride a trike, by gum!

He'd ride to Mrs Chicken's — then

He'd ride back home to Mum.

At nearly four years old, he found

That reading could be fun

A few words here, a few words there

And soon a book was done.

And when our lad was nearly five

A bicycle he rode

Around and round the garden

And never squashed one toad.

At nearly six the bold intrepid

Iain conquered French.

(The language, that is, not the country)

And I have to ment-

ion that, when he was nearly seven

New Math was the thing,

He worked till he could do each one.

And oh! How he could sing!

When nearly eight his first football

Became a great delight.

He'd play with it at lunchtime

And even on Christmas night.

When nearly nine he found the time

To write some super stories

Some about his animals

And some of heroes' glories.

And now the boy has grown so tall

A prince among all men.

He isn't nearly anything

He is exactly   TEN!!!

Song Lyrics

Photo - Betty Ortiz

The singing beetle

One day I was driving along in my car

Listening to Radio 1

The music wasn't my cup of tea

So I turned over to Radio 3

Hoping to find a Symphony

To set my blues on the run.

And as I drove along in my car

Listening to Radio 3

A man was discussing creatures so queer

You'd never imagine in many a year

And as his words penetrated my ears

I heard him describing someone like me.

Now there are insects that squeak

There are beetles that squawk

And spiders whose eyes wave

Around on a stalk

There are bright little spark bugs

Glow in the dark bugs

Smilingly mean bugs

Highly unclean bugs

All creatures you'd sooner not

See on your fork.

And there's one little bug called

The Ironclad Beetle,

A creature of habit, so dull and so small

That if you saw it

You'd simply ignore it

You wouldn't record it

Or snap it or draw it

No likes and no followers to record it

And the experts decreed she had

No voice at all. (WHAT?)

But in total defiance

Of the bold men of Science

The Ironclad Beetle sings out

Loud and clear

A sweet little song

Not too loud, not too long

If nobody heard

Was that so absurd?

For she sings for herself

Not for anyone else

All alone, on one day of each year.

Oh yes, on one day each year

She will sing without fear

You may jest, you may jeer

She just doesn't care.

For she sings for herself

Not for anyone else

And if you don't want to hear

She won't

Shed a tear.

    (The Beetle Sings a verse)

Oh yes on one day each year

She will sing without fear

You may jest, you may jeer

She just doesn't care.

For she sings for herself

Not for anyone else

And if you do want to hear

You'll have to wait...

Until next year.

Sometimes I think

Sometimes I think I'm hungry, but

Maybe I'm just tired

Sometimes I think I'm angry, but

Maybe I'm just wired.

Sometimes I think I'm lost

Maybe I'm just out of touch

And if I think that I've been crossed

I find it all a bit too much.

The world is spinning out of shape

We sit and watch with mouths agape

Let's slow the pace right down

Play it cool, lose the frown.

Sometimes I think I'm on a roll

But maybe I'm just movin'.

Sometimes I think we're in a hole

But maybe we're just groovin'.

Sometimes I think I'm being watched

But maybe I'm just vain.

Sometimes I know I'm being watched
But maybe I'm a bit insane.

The world is spinning out of shape
And it's too late for gaffer tape
Let's slow the pace right down -
Play it cool, lose the frown.

Sometimes I think I'd like to start
A brand new revolution
Flip the planet upside down
To clean off the pollution.
Sometimes I think we need to shake
Humanity's foundation
Stir the pot to blend one bright new
Multi-flavoured nation.

The earth is spinning patiently
Among the stars so graciously
Let's slow the pace right down
Stop fooling round.

Sometimes I think I'll wait and see

What new thoughts lie in store for me.

Thinking is a mystery

I'd like to think for eternity

You're welcome to think

Along with me...

The comeback queen gives herself a jolly good talking to

(dedicated to anyone who has ever endured a 'cattle call' audition)

My heart is pumping madly

And it's going to my head.

My stomach cramps

I'm breathing badly

In a minute I'll be dead.

I want to die before it starts

Don't let me die up there instead.

Why, why do I do it?

Why do I put myself through it?

Try as I might, I can't do it right

I should give up the fight

[*After all, who am I fighting but me, myself and I?*]

I knew the rules when I started

My fault if I'm getting down-hearted.

I've been here before

I know the score

I can make it once more.

[*There now, all you needed was a good talking to*]

You don't want money—

So you say

You don't want fame—

Not right away.

You don't want lovers—

Well, maybe just one

One would be fun

Not too young

But still handsome.

What is it, makes me carry on?

What is this strange disease?

Pushing me out into

The big bad world

Of heartache, rejection

And nasty little sleazy men

Who don't know their arts

From their Antipodes!

Please! Let me have faith

There's no point in wanting

And hoping and needing

Unless I can keep myself

Wholly believing in me.

That's the way it must be - It must be.

Some folk believe in nothing but work

Others in nothing but fate.

I'd like to say that the will has a way

Of working for those who don't hesitate.

The power of positive thinking

Is stronger than anything seems.

When you think of a deed, as a deed, indeed

You're halfway to living your dreams.

[*And if you believe that you'll believe anything. However -*]

Dreams have a funny way of coming true.

Don't try to make it

Unless you can take it

All the way through.

Don't hitch your

Wagon to a star

Unless you've an excellent

Head — and voice — for heights

You may be carried too far

Out of mind, out of sight...

                                      Stick to your

Life of fantasy, safely cocooned from the

Real live world. But if you want a

Chance to see how the grown-ups live

Something's gotta give...

Why, why do I do it?

Why do I put myself through it?

Try as I might I can't do it right

I should give up the fight

Only – maybe - not tonight!

A loving hold

I'm feeling sleepy

And maybe slightly drunk, but I can't sleep.

Tonight was such a night—

I could have climbed a mountain

I could weep.

Tonight I stood alone, yet not so lonely

For the company I keep

Keeps a loving hold on me.

I think of all the things I've ever done

And it seems clear

That all I was, the child, the girl the woman

They're all here

For Time is just a river flowing round me

And though I change each year

What I was

Is always near.

The little dancing kid with

Sequins on her dress and in her hair

The girl who sang her heart out loud

When no-one was there

The winner of the Shakespeare prize

To be or not to be

Without a prayer

Keep me in their loving care.

Tonight a dream fell out of bed

Became reality

A dream so wrapped around my heart

And in my head, I couldn't see

That all I ever wanted

Was within me

For the dream, when free

Keeps a loving hold on me.

Merry go round of life
a stoical lullaby

Introduction

Welcome to the playground

I'm so glad you're here

This world that you've arrived in

Might not be here next year.

There's lots to entertain you

For as long as it lasts

Take a turn at all the games before

They slip into the past.

The swings will take you

From low to high

Get you accustomed to

Earth and sky.

On the climbing frame

You can just hang around

Right way up or upside down.

The slip'rpy slide looks scary at first

But once you've come down it

You'll know that the worst thing

About it is doing it over and over and

Over and over and over again

While the seesaw is more of the same.

Repetition is the name of the game.

Forwards and backwards and side to side

In and out just like the tide–

But if you're more of the circular kind

And the merry-go-round is on your mind…

Don't worry, don't panic, don't fret

There's no need to be upset.

This playground of life

Where you've come to stay

Is the merry-go-round of

Day after week after month after year–

And there's nothing to fear.

You just need to hear

The instructions that I'll

Whisper in your

Cute little ear….

(Are you ready? – Here we go ☺

Live in the moment

That's all we've got.

Enjoy what's around you

The past will confound you

The future astound you, coz it's

It's either what you hoped for

Or it's not.

What's gone won't be changed

Though it might be forgotten.

You can't exchange it

Or even rearrange it.

What's to come is no less

Than a gift you can't guess.

It's either what you hoped for

Or it's not.

Make the most of what you've got

Stay in the here and now.

You're only meant to be here

Until your final bow.

That tightrope that you're walking

Is supporting you, not thwarting you.

Whether it's fun or terrifying

If you believe you're really flying…

Use your toes to get a grip

To remind you, if you slip

Not to hold on too tightly

Don't be frightened to let go

Your future is already here, and it's

Either what you hoped for

Or it's not.

Make the most of what you've got

Stay in the here and now

You're only meant to be here

Until your final bow

That tightrope that you're walking

Is supporting you, not thwarting you.

Whether it's fun or terrifying

If you believe you're really flying –

Use your toes to get a grip

To remind you, if you slip

Not to hold on too tightly

Don't be frightened to let go –

It's the paradox of existence

There's no point in resistance

Coz... Your future is already here

And it's either what you hoped for

Or it's not.

The good old days

In days of old, so I've been told

Each man was an honest worker

When you got a job you shut your gob

And no-one was a shirker.

The dole queue reached a mile or more

There was nothing in the larder

The beer was strong though food was scarce

And people worked so much harder.

    That's the story we were told

    That's the lie that we were sold

    No use shedding tears

    Nothing changes through the years.

The old folks crack that a few years back

They had just and honest bosses

You worked all day for your two bob pay

Less, if the boss had losses.

But things are so much brighter now

With the Unions taking over

We can rest assured that our jobs are safe

And we'll all live in clover.

    That's the story we were told

    That's the lie that we were sold

    No use shedding tears

    Nothing changes through the years.

My grandma went to church on Sundays

Grateful for her Saviour

She cooked and washed for the old man's boss

And thanked him for the favour.

Now she waits for her tomb in a bed-sit room

With a gas ring for a fire

Her pension pays for the good old days

While the rent keeps getting higher.

    That's the story we were told

    That's the lie that we were sold

    No use shedding tears

    Nothing changes through the years.

When I've had my day and my hair is grey

And I'm sitting in my wheelchair

I've paid my stamps and taxes so

I'm certain of my welfare.

My kids'll ask me about my past

I think I've a mind to tell them

How I had no choice to raise my voice

To avoid all the ills that befell them.

My kids for sure will call me a bore

And think they've all the answers

And I'll think of the time of me youth and me prime

And of all the wasted chances.

> That's the story we were told
>
> That's the lie that we were sold
>
> No use shedding tears
>
> Nothing changes through the years.

Where the old folk go

What am I doing? Here I go again.

It's not the same as last time

I can't remember when.

What am I doing? I've been here before.

It was somewhere else. Who's keeping score?

What am I doing? Stop while I'm ahead.

Whatever I was about to do,

Do something else instead.

I'm tired of being grouchy. I'm tired of being poor.

Found the root of the problem. Don't run any more.

I don't know where to go

Whether I'm in or out of the flow

All I know is I don't want to go

Where the Old Folk Go.

Maybe I'm sad. Maybe I'm mad

Maybe I've lost the right to be bad.

Every day is a dumb replay

Of things I used to know.

There's no reason I can find

For going round in circles inside my mind.

Outside the window life goes on

Frantic, casual, shouted and sung

People are cruel. People are kind

Sometimes reasons result in rhymes.

And I still don't know why I go

Onwards and backwards over and over

Getting dumped in the Undertow

Coming up for air--ever so slowly.

Should I go – where? I don't know, there

Has to be some place I'll never outgrow

Maybe it's nearby, maybe in time I'll

Understand why it's so

That I'll never compliantly go

Where the Old Folk Go.

The bottom line

Once upon a time not so long ago

A bunch of people thought they'd have a go

At making loads of money fast and easy.

Oh yeah!

Easy peazy was the song they sang

Trading other people's debts

With joyful abandon

Riding high with no regrets above

The Bottom Line.

(and they sang)

 Don't break the rules just bend them a bit

If it goes wrong the banks'll take the hit.

Our future's bright and breezy, when we're

Riding high above

The Bottom Line.

And though it wasn't a crime - as such

There is only ever so much

Money in the world to be found
Above The Bottom Line.

Or wealth-creating bobs and bits
Above the ground or down in the pits
The only ones who'll be in the shit
Will be those losers below
The Bottom Line.

(and they sang)
Don't break the rules just bend them a bit
If it goes wrong the government'll take the hit.
Our future's bright and breezy, when we're
Riding high above
The Bottom Line.

So once upon a time not so long ago
We all discovered just how low
Some folk will go to grab power and control of
The Bottom Line.

But we don't need a hero

To save us from this mess

We just need to be the very best that

We can be, then we can help the rest

To rise above The Bottom Line.

(and we sing)

Don't break the rules just bend them a bit

It won't go wrong when we all commit

We'll be bright and breezy

When we take charge of

The Bottom Line.

We don't need a revolution

That's just going round and round and round,

We need a solution that will

Shake the foundations of society,

Flip it upside down.

So come on people, join with me

It's time to sing a chorus of unity

Coz nobody wins as long as anyone is left

Below the Bottom Line.

AND WE SING

Don't break the rules just bend them a bit

It won't go wrong when we all commit

We'll be bright and breezy when

We take charge of

The Bottom Line.

Australia Fair no more

a parody on Peter Dodds McCormick's *poem of 1878, "Advance Australia Fair", the Australian national anthem.*

Australians all, let's not rejoice

We're neither young nor free

Our golden soil and wealth are all

Stained with shame and misery.

Our land abounds with nature's gifts

That we're afraid to share

Let history's page record our rage

For the loss of Australia Fair.

When Reza died,

And our government lied

We fell into despair.

In sorrowful strains then

Let us mourn for

The loss of Australia Fair.

Beneath the radiant Southern Cross

We've toiled with heart and hand

To make this Commonwealth of ours

A fair and decent land.

For those who come across the seas

We've boundless plains to spare

Unless, of course, you arrive by boat

Then Australia isn't there.

When Faysal died,

And our government lied

'Twas more than we could bear.

Let history's page

Record our rage

For the loss of Australia Fair.

When Hamid died,

When Omid died

When Fazel died,

When Rakib died

When Faysel died,

When Reza died

A stench was in the air.

In sorrowful strains then let us mourn

For the loss of Australia Fair.

Except–

It never actually existed in the first place

It was all an illusion.

In memory, and in honour of these people who sought refuge in Australia, and found rejection, torture and death.

Reza Berati, Faysal Ishak Ahmed, Hamid Kehazae, Rakib Khan, Omid Masoumali, Fazel Chegeni

And there are many, many more...

When I was a little girl
(to the tune of Kingston Hill)

Oh when I was a little girl

That's when the earth was young

Many a girlish dream I dreamed

And I had me praises sung.

They told me I was pretty

But I knew that they lied

Coz what I saw in the mirror was what

I felt like inside.

Chorus:

With me toora-lassie,

Whack-the- lassie

Toora Loora Lay.

And when I was a teenager

That's when the days were long

Many a teenage dream I dreamt

And I had me praises sung.

They said that I was clever
But not quite clever enough
To do the things I dreamed about
Just other boring stuff.

With me toora-lassie
Whack-the- lassie
Toora Loora Lay.

And when I was a young woman
That's when the days were sweet
With wifely chores and motherhood
I thought my life complete.
I dreamed of raising heroes
Who would save the world, and me
Who knew that hero acorns
Would not fall far from the tree.

With me toora-lassie,
Whack-the- lassie
Toora Loora Lay.

And as I passed through middle-age

That's when the days were strong

I found what I was good at

And I had me praises sung.

My girlhood dreams came closer

And for a few short years

I strived to make the best of it

Without favour or fear.

With me toora-lassie,

Whack-the- lassie

Toora Loora Lay.

And now I'm in my senior years

The days are very short

My attention span's even shorter

And my dreams've come to naught.

And while I might seem cynical

Of all my life to date

When it comes to my two hero sons

I reckon it's not too late.

Oh when I was a little girl

That's when the earth was young

Many a girlish deed I did

And I had my praises sung.

I fought with life ten thousand times

And always lost but then

The earth would turn and I would learn

To fight all over again.

With me toora-lassie

Whack-the- lassie

Toora

Loora

Lay—ee-yay-ee-yay-ee-yay-ay-ay!

Sunsets and kites

There used to be sunsets.

There used to be golden days fading to grey

A sky full of light

Would fight with the night

For the right to die.

And there used to be rainbows.

There used to be high class hues of indigo blues

A colourful crown

Reaching down to the ground

Where gold could be found.

    Memory plays some funny tricks

    Fooling in your mind.

    You know you've been here before

    But not like this

    There was so much more.

There used to be flowers

There used to be perfumed trees

That moved in the breeze

And creatures with wings

They'd whistle and sing

Such beautiful things.

    Memory plays some funny tricks

    Fooling in your mind.

    You know you've been here before

    But not like this

    There was so much more.

There used to be sunsets.

There used to be flaming skies scarlet with sighs.

There used to be light

The world was so bright

Now there's just night...

And a child with a kite.

Alternative ending, depending on how it all goes...
And it's past putting right.

About the Author

Anton Mellor Photography

Flloyd Kennedy, Australian-born Liverpool-based actress, singer-songwriter, writer, director and voice, speech and accent coach, travelled to the UK in the late 1960s where she took part in the British folk revival. She performed street theatre, cabaret and fringe theatre in Scotland throughout the 1980s and 90s, then returned to Australia where she undertook research into the performing voice (specifically Shakespeare) for her doctorate. Back in the UK since 2015, Flloyd performs, directs, writes and teaches voice, accent and acting skills at colleges and universities in the UK, US and Australia. Through her private studio Being in Voice she coaches student and professional actors, private individuals and community and corporate groups. She is artistic director of Thunder's Mouth Theatre (theatre of poetry, passion and philosophy).

The songs are available on all major music streaming sites, including Spotify, Apple Music and Amazon Prime, as well as
Bandcamp: https://flloydwith2ells.bandcamp.com/releases

Acknowledgements

With much gratitude to the kind friends and colleagues who have patiently encouraged and supported me through various drafts on the way to publication, including Susannah Finzi,,Morag Stark, Judi Lehrhaupt, Allana Noyes, Margi Brown Ash, Ira Seidenstein, and to Terry Cripps for the beautiful cover image.